LIGHTNING BOLT BOOKS™

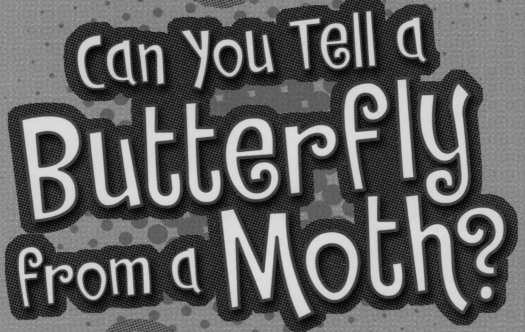

Can You Tell a Butterfly from a Moth?

Buffy Silverman

Lerner Publications Company
Minneapolis

To Emma.
Spread your bright
wings and soar!

Lerner Publications Company
A division of Lerner Publishing Group, Inc.
241 First Avenue North
Minneapolis, MN 55401 U.S.A.

Website address: www.lernerbooks.com

Library of Congress Cataloging-in-Publication Data

Silverman, Buffy.
　　Can you tell a butterfly from a moth? / by Buffy Silverman.
　　　　p. cm. — (Lightning bolt books™—animal look-alikes)
　　Includes index.
　　ISBN 978-0-7613-6731-4 (lib. bdg. : alk. paper)
　　1. Butterflies—Juvenile literature. 2. Moths—Juvenile literature. I. Title.
　QL544.2.S496 2012
　　595.78—dc22   2010050812

Manufactured in the United States of America
1 — CG — 7/15/11

Contents

Bright Wings or Dull Wings?

Butterflies and moths look alike in many ways. Adult butterflies and moths have four wings. The wings are covered with tiny scales. Scales give the wings their colors.

This giant swallowtail butterfly's bright wings make it easy to spot.

Both butterflies and moths are insects. Adult insects have six legs. Many adult insects also have wings. One way to tell butterflies and moths apart is to look at their wings. Most butterfly wings are brightly colored. Moth wings usually have dull colors. They are often gray or brown.

This Zale moth blends into the places where it lives. It is hard to find.

There are many more kinds
of moths than butterflies. But
you might notice butterflies
more often. Butterflies
fly during the day.

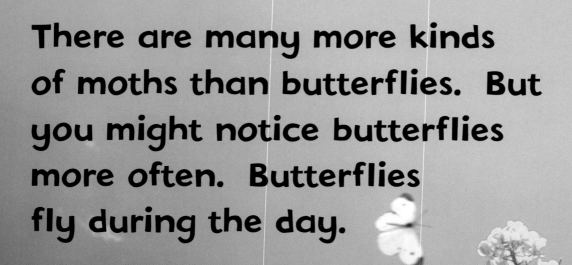

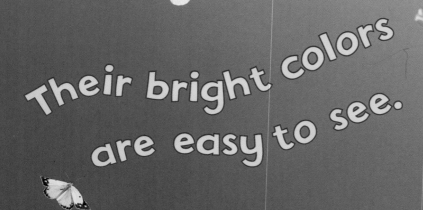

Their bright colors
are easy to see.

Moths rest during the day.
They usually fly at night.
Their dull colors make them
hard to see then. Look near a
porch light on a summer night.
Do you see moths flying
around the light?

Most moths are nocturnal. This means they are active at night.

Wings Up or Wings Out?

A butterfly lands on a flower. The butterfly folds its wings up. That's the way butterflies rest.

Butterflies, such as this painted lady, fold their wings when they rest.

A moth lands on a tree trunk. The moth spreads its wings flat when it rests.

Wings are attached to the middle part of an insect's body. A butterfly's body is skinny.

This swallowtail butterfly has a skinny body.

Thick hairs cover a moth's body. It looks fat and fuzzy.

This giant peacock moth has a thick body.

Sensing the World

Insects have antennas. Insects use their antennas to feel, taste, and smell. Look at the tips of this butterfly's antennas. Butterfly antennas have round knobs at the ends.

Most moth antennas do not have knobs. The tips are thin and pointed. Some moth antennas look like feathers.

This moth has long, thin antennas. The tips are pointed, without knobs.

Butterflies and moths wave their antennas. Their antennas smell flowers.

Then the butterflies and moths fly to the sweet-smelling flowers to find food.

A moth waves its feathery antennas. It smells other moths. Moths and butterflies find their mates by smelling with their antennas.

A male gypsy moth has feathery antennas.

Finding Food

This butterfly flits through a garden. Sun shines on its colorful wings.

The butterfly lands on a flower and folds its wings. Then the butterfly unrolls a long tube and pushes it into a flower. The tube is the butterfly's mouth. The butterfly sips a sweet liquid called nectar from the flower.

A butterfly uses its tube-shaped mouth to drink from flowers.

Later, the sun sets. A dark moth flies through a field. The moth's wings are hard to see.

This moth waves its antennas and smells something sweet. It lands on a flower. It spreads its wings. Then it unrolls its tube. The moth sips nectar from the flower.

A moth drinks from a flower the same way a butterfly does.

Growing Up

All insects begin life as an egg. What hatches from a butterfly or moth egg? **A caterpillar!**

This luna moth caterpillar just hatched from its egg.

A caterpillar chews leaves. It eats and grows. Soon it grows too big for its skin. The caterpillar molts. **That means it sheds its old skin.** It has a new skin underneath. The caterpillar molts many times as it grows.

This monarch butterfly caterpillar is shedding its skin.

Finally, the caterpillar is finished growing. Then the moth caterpillar hides under leaves or soil. The caterpillar spins a cocoon. The cocoon is made of silk. It covers the caterpillar.

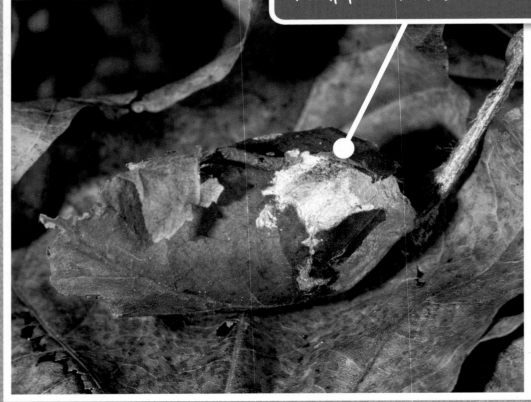

This moth is tightly wrapped in its cocoon.

Inside the cocoon, the caterpillar sheds its skin again. It grows four wings and six long legs. The caterpillar changes into a moth.

This cocoon is cut away to show the moth changing inside.

A butterfly caterpillar does not spin a cocoon. The caterpillar climbs to a leaf or branch. Then it spins a strong silk button.

The button holds the caterpillar to the leaf. The caterpillar hangs upside down. Then it molts.

This monarch caterpillar is molting.

A hard shell called a chrysalis covers the caterpillar. Inside the chrysalis, the caterpillar changes into a butterfly.

Butterflies and moths fly in gardens, meadows, and woods. Can you tell these look-alikes apart?

Who Am I?

Look at the pictures below. Which ones are butterflies? Which ones are moths?

 I spin a cocoon before I change into an adult.

My chrysalis is attached to a leaf.

 I fold my wings up when I rest.

I spread my wings flat when I rest.

 My wings are brightly colored.

My wings have dull colors.

Fun Facts

- Look at the spots on this moth's wings. They look like owl eyes. The spots fool some creatures that eat moths. The creatures think they see the eyes of an owl, so they flee!

- Some caterpillars also trick hunting birds and insects. This tiger swallowtail caterpillar looks a lot like bird poop. Hungry creatures leave it alone.

- An older tiger swallowtail caterpillar has spots on its back. The spots look like big eyes. A hungry critter might think it is a snake and fly away.

- Monarch butterflies taste bad. So birds and other animals learn to avoid these colorful insects.

Glossary

antenna: an organ on an insect's head that the insect uses to feel, taste, and smell

caterpillar: a young butterfly or moth. Caterpillars eat plants and grow quickly.

chrysalis: the hard shell that protects a caterpillar as it changes into a butterfly

cocoon: the case of silk that covers and protects a moth caterpillar as it changes from a caterpillar into a moth

insect: an animal that has six legs and three main body parts as an adult

molt: to shed old skin

nectar: a sweet liquid made by flowers

scale: a plate that gives color to the wings of butterflies and moths